Complete this neon chequered pattern by filling the page with squares!

I'm feeling square-eyed!

Add more sunflowers to this field!

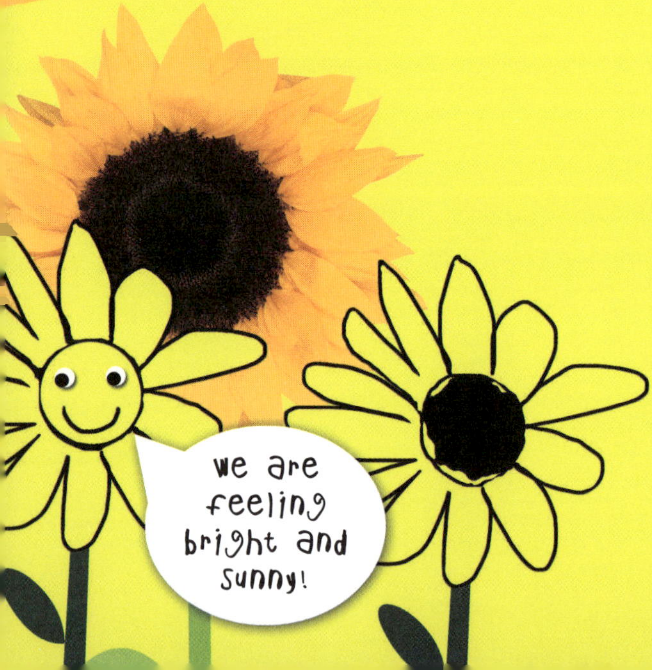

Fill the page with more neon triangles.

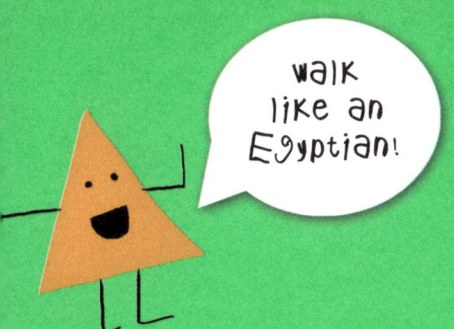

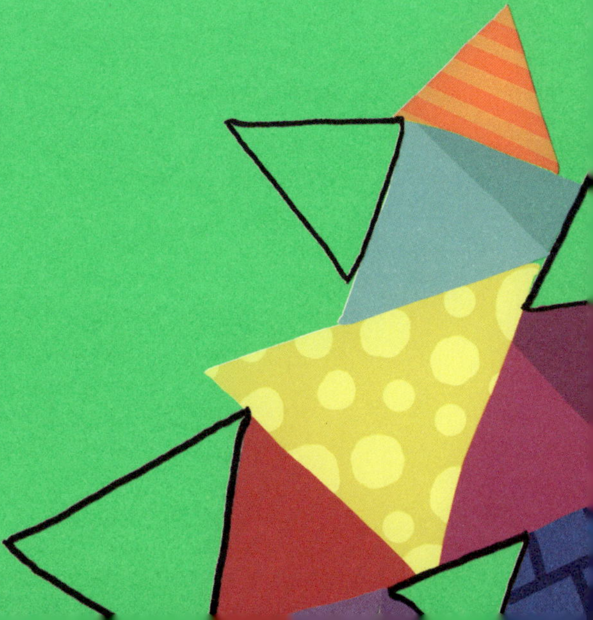

Doodle the superheroes that own these disguises!

who is the owner of this giant green moustache?

Doodle the owner of these pink eyes.

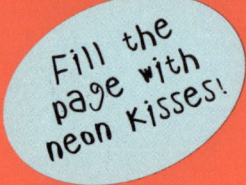

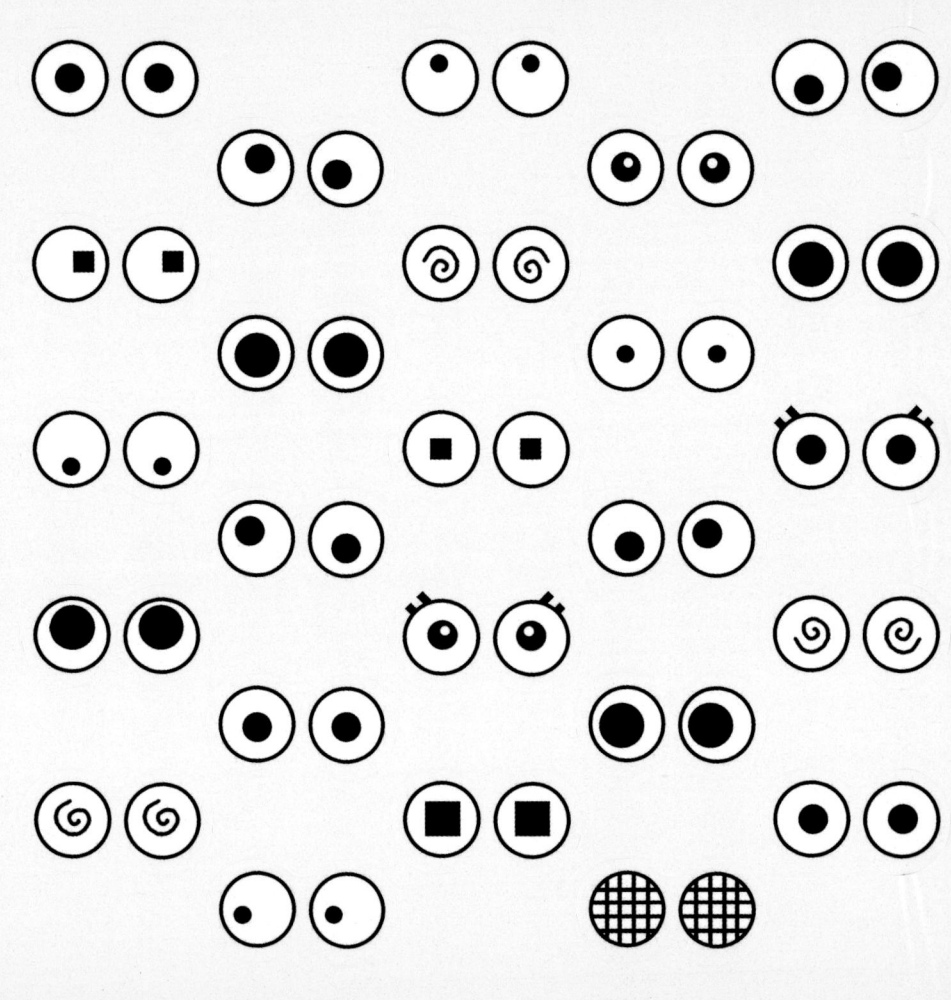

Turn this neon circle into a bouncy basketball.

Fancy a game?

Doodle the owners of these crazy hairstyles!

I'm a punk rocker!

Turn this pumpkin into a scary jack-o'-lantern.

"My name is Jack!"

Doodle more neon bright lightbulbs.

King of the world!

Add jewels to this bright crown.

Add lots of faces to these neon circles.

Add a pattern to the clouds.

Add a face to this giant scary pea.

who is driving the big truck?

Who wears these neon green spectacles?

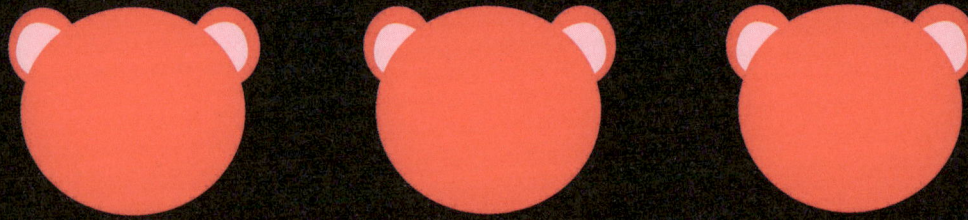

Keep drawing around the heart!

This is a masterpiece in pink!

What has Monsieur paintbrush painted?

Doodle some musical notes coming from the pink radio!

What's playing on Monster Radio today?